SAMUEL KEMP

MANIPULATION

Mastering the Art of Persuasion, Recognizing Manipulation, and Guarding Your Mind
(2024)

Contents

1

INTRODUCTION

The human mind is undeniably intricate, serving as the foundation of our individual identities, preferences, and interactions with the world. It shapes our behavior, motivations, and unique personalities. Despite this complexity, there is an underlying predictability to the human mind, a common thread that unites us. Humans possess a remarkable adaptability, making it possible to influence them in subtle ways without their awareness. Manipulation can take many forms, from tweaking your words to altering your body language and adjusting your communication style, all of which can shape people's responses.

This concept isn't groundbreaking. If you're in sales, you've likely been trained in framing responses to encourage purchases. Teachers are taught to create effective learning environments for children, and those in law enforcement learn how body language can convey dominance. In essence, your actions, words, and demeanor can determine how others react. This ability hinges on the fact that, although people can think and act independently, much of their behavior and emotions are unconsciously influenced.

By tapping into the unconscious mind, you gain the power to control others. You can steer their thoughts, and by doing so, you can influence their actions. This book will be your guide in this process. You'll delve into the world of manipulation as a form of social influence, exploring what it is and its ethical dimensions. While manipulation itself isn't inherently good or bad, its use can have positive or negative effects on others. You'll learn effective manipulation techniques and delve into the role of emotions in this process. Various forms of emotional manipulation will be explored, along with different methods to exert influence.

Specifically, we'll focus on emotional manipulation to enhance your ability to shape behaviors. You'll also learn about mind control techniques that genuinely affect how people interact. Neuro-Linguistic Programming, a method that taps into the unconscious mind, will be explained. You'll discover the power of persuasion and how it can aid you in controlling others subtly. Lastly, you'll explore the impact of body language and posture on your ability to influence people.

Mastering the art of influencing and controlling others can be highly beneficial. It enables you to guide individuals toward decisions that benefit them. By influencing others, you can ensure that you maintain control over situations. If you know someone is prone to harmful decisions, you can influence them positively, as doctors do with treatment options or salespeople do with product choices. This book equips you with the skills to accomplish just that.

However, it's crucial to remember that the actions of others are a reflection of how you encourage them to behave. Your approach directly influences their actions. While you can shape their behavior, it's essential to respect their thoughts and autonomy. If you choose to manipulate others, you must also accept the associated risks and consequences. Sometimes, though, the benefits may outweigh the risks, and if you believe that's the case, it becomes your prerogative.

2

WHAT IS MANIPULATION?

Have you ever experienced a moment when you fervently desired the ability to influence the actions of others? Maybe you were in a situation where you desperately sought to find a way to persuade someone to assist you. Alternatively, you might have wished to guide someone towards making choices that you believed were in their best interest. Regardless of the motive, you may have strongly yearned for the power to exert control over another individual.

It's entirely feasible to achieve this – acquiring the skills to guide and manage individuals isn't as daunting as you might have first imagined. The art of persuasion enables you to effectively shape others' actions. This skill empowers you to influence people's behavior in various ways, convincing them to act according to your wishes. Moreover, it has the potential to alter the thought processes of others, essentially reshaping their minds.

In this chapter, you will delve deeper into the concept of manipulation. You will gain insights into its role as a means of exerting social influence, and you will explore prevalent motives behind individuals' decisions to manipulate those in their vicinity. As you progress through this chapter, remember that it lays the foundational knowledge required to comprehend the manifestations and mechanisms of manipulation. You will also grasp the frequently employed rationales for manipulating others.

Social Influence and Manipulation

In essence, manipulation serves as a means of exerting social influence. Social influence, at its core, denotes the natural inclination of individuals to adapt their actions and conduct based on the prevailing social context. Yielding to social influence entails a probable alteration in one's behavior in reaction to external stimuli. This adjustment may arise as a response to requests or statements made by others, be prompted by the conduct of others, or result from one's perception of the expectations and actions of those in their immediate social milieu.

In broad terms, there exist three fundamental approaches to exerting social influence. These encompass compliance, identification, and internalization. While each method operates with its unique nuances, they all tap into two inherent human desires—the desire to be accurate and the desire to be accepted. We will delve into these aspects more extensively in subsequent discussions.

Conformity

Conformity involves outwardly adhering to a directive or rule without genuine endorsement of it in principle. Consider a scenario where you're instructed to implement a workplace policy change, such as refusing service to individuals wearing purple and green attire simultaneously. Even if you find this rule arbitrary or inappropriate, you enforce it simply because it's an order from your employer, believing that you must adhere to it to keep your job. Consequently, you inform customers that they cannot enter your store based on the colors of their clothing. You explain your disagreement with the rule but express your lack of choice in following it, driven by the need to meet financial obligations and provide for your family. This exemplifies conformity—acting as if you're in accord, even when your true convictions contradict the matter at hand.

Internalization

Internalization, conversely, aims to shape both the way individuals think and behave simultaneously. It involves the endeavor to alter someone else's thoughts while also motivating them to modify their actions. Essentially, it entails persuading people to align with your own thoughts and convictions, prompting them to shift their thinking and actions concurrently. Consider this scenario: you are requested to reconsider your belief in a particular action you've been engaged in. For instance, you may have been informed that eating meat is prohibited during work hours, and simultaneously, your manager has provided you with information about the rationale behind avoiding meat altogether. If you were to acknowledge the validity of these reasons and consequently adjust your behavior by refraining from consuming meat, you have internalized the message – you now believe that abstaining from meat consumption is the right course of action, leading to a change in your habits.

Identification

Identification sets itself apart from the other two forms of social influence in a distinctive way. It hinges on the inherent tendency of individuals to be swayed by those they hold in high regard. When someone admires another person, be it a celebrity or anyone else, a natural inclination arises to align their thoughts and beliefs with those of the admired figure. Consequently, when individuals relate to someone they admire, they invariably strive to imitate them. In essence, imitation serves as a profound manifestation of flattery, and by mimicking a celebrity or a revered individual, one unquestionably succumbs to their influence.

Manipulation

In essence, manipulation entails altering another person's thoughts, emotions, or actions without their awareness. It involves the ability to modify someone's behavior, essentially guiding their actions and exerting a direct influence over them. Manipulation strives to prompt the individual to alter their thoughts or conduct, typically employing methods that are often perceived as indirect or misleading. Since manipulation hinges on keeping the other person unaware of the manipulation process, it can rapidly prove highly effective by evading detection and facilitating manipulative actions.

The key characteristic of manipulation is its dependency on the manipulated individual remaining unaware of the manipulation taking place. This is frequently accomplished through hidden forms of aggression, although there are exceptions. Manipulation may occasionally be employed to benefit the manipulator, although this is not always the case. It can also occasionally have detrimental effects on the person being manipulated, although this is not always the outcome.

Motivations for Manipulation

In essence, individuals resort to manipulation when their objective is to instigate alterations either in someone's actions or in their thoughts. Several driving factors underpin this behavior, but the ultimate outcome remains quite consistent – the desire to influence another person. Whether it's to prompt an individual to modify their conduct for a specific purpose or to encourage a shift in their mindset, manipulation serves as the means to attain these goals. As you delve into this section, you'll discern varying degrees of subtlety among these motivations. The most prevalent reasons for manipulating others encompass the following:

1. Pursuit of personal gain:

Certain individuals exhibit a comfort level in exploiting others, treating those in their proximity as mere stepping stones to advance in life effortlessly. These individuals typically lack empathy and perceive others as either instruments to be controlled or as targets to exploit, solely for their personal advancement.

2. Hunger for power:

Some people harbor an insatiable need for supremacy to feel secure within themselves. They intentionally manipulate others not out of necessity but to wield power over them for their own gratification. This dangerous mindset disregards the well-being of others, with no qualms about causing harm. They believe that the sense of tranquility they derive from this exercise justifies their actions.

3. Desire for control:

Similar to the thirst for power, certain individuals manipulate others to maintain control over their surroundings. They feel a sense of stability and composure only when they exert this level of dominance over those around them. Consequently, it becomes common to witness individuals seeking to control others in order to alleviate their own anxiety, even if it means manipulating someone else.

4. For amusement:

Some individuals simply indulge in manipulation as a form of entertainment, often stemming from boredom or a desire to break the monotony of life. They turn manipulation into a game, challenging themselves to interact with others in unconventional ways, such as coaxing someone into performing an action simply to see if they can.

5. Unintentionally:

Some people inadvertently manipulate others, driven by their inability to connect with the emotions of those around them. They usually don't harbor any deliberate intention to manipulate but find themselves doing so due to issues with self-control, self-awareness, and a deficiency in empathy.

6. Impulsively:

For some, manipulation is a spontaneous act devoid of premeditation. They engage in it impulsively, lacking the forethought or planning associated with manipulation. These individuals aren't necessarily malevolent; their manipulative actions often serve as a reaction to preserve their self-image, which would otherwise be tarnished by their impulsive behaviors.

7. Covert agendas:

Occasionally, manipulation occurs with a distinct purpose – to steer someone toward actions that align with a concealed agenda. A classic example is scam phone calls, where manipulators target vulnerable individuals, persuading them to carry out specific tasks or purchase gift cards, all to further their ulterior motives.

3

THE ETHICS OF MANIPULATION

Consider this scenario: You find yourself in a conversation with your closest friend, who passionately expresses her deep dislike for her boyfriend. She despises every aspect of their relationship, yet she adamantly refuses to end it. In this situation, is it ethically justifiable to exert significant influence on her to persuade her to break up with him? This question elicits diverse responses.

Ultimately, the ethical dimension of manipulation is a complex matter, subject to contextual variables. When contemplating the act of manipulating someone, one may grapple with questions of moral permissibility. The answer hinges largely on intent.

It is essential to recognize that manipulation, in and of itself, is a neutral tool, akin to a firearm or any other instrument. It bears no inherent moral quality; it is not inherently virtuous, nor is it inherently malevolent. Assessing the morality of manipulation necessitates an examination of the motivations behind it. Of course, there are those who assert that manipulation is inherently unethical, as is often the case with various subjects. Some individuals argue that substances like alcohol, tobacco, and even caffeine are universally detrimental and should be avoided at all costs. However, the reality is far more nuanced. The assessment of any action or practice depends on individual perspectives, rather than unanimous agreement.

Consider this perspective: If you possess knowledge that someone intends to commit a mass shooting but have the ability to manipulate them into abandoning their deadly plans, is it morally wrong to do so? Is it unethical to employ this skill for a noble cause, preventing harm to others? Conversely, is it wrong to manipulate someone out of sheer boredom?

In such cases, one must weigh the greater good of their actions. Taking an extreme stance is inadequate because, like most intricate subjects, the ethics of manipulation fall along a spectrum. It is neither intrinsically virtuous nor inherently wicked; instead, the intentions behind the manipulation must be scrutinized. This involves considering the trustworthiness of others' actions, the potential harm caused by one's behavior, and various other factors.

Some individuals misuse manipulation for wrongful or malicious purposes, exploiting their skills to gain power or coerce others into unethical actions, such as financial scams. These manipulators disregard the well-being of their targets and show no inclination to confront or reconcile with the morality of their actions. What matters to them is achieving their objectives at any cost.

Nonetheless, there are instances where manipulation can be morally justified. When the greater good is served, one must evaluate whether their actions hold value. Manipulation might, for example, prevent harm to multiple individuals or deter someone from pursuing a path detrimental to their own interests. Recognizing the merit in these actions is crucial.

Ultimately, manipulation remains a morally ambiguous practice. Arguments can be made both for and against its acceptability, regardless of the potential to save lives or improve outcomes. Those engaged in this debate must possess the mental fortitude to navigate its complexities.

Manipulation inherently involves deception and subterfuge. If one deems deception and underhanded tactics unacceptable, manipulation may not align with their values. Those uncomfortable with interacting with others in ways that go unnoticed may prefer alternative methods of influence, such as persuasion or non-verbal communication, which do not carry the same degree of deceit.

Ultimately, the determination of ethics falls to the individual. However, it is important to note that manipulating others for personal gain, inflicting harm on them, or engaging in actions that could lead to legal consequences should be approached with caution. Manipulation diminishes another person's autonomy, setting it apart from persuasion, which preserves their ability to choose freely. When manipulating someone, you provide the illusion of choice while strategically altering their behavior by leveraging an understanding of cognitive processes. Recognizing this infringement upon their inherent rights as individuals is essential when weighing the pros and cons of manipulation.

4

HOW TO MANIPULATE EFFECTIVELY

Now that we've clarified the ethical aspects and our comprehension of manipulation, it's time to delve into the crucial intricacies. In this chapter, we will explore the components that contribute to successful manipulation. This chapter's emphasis will be on the methods for influencing and altering the thoughts and behaviors of others. We will guide you through the three essential criteria that must be met for manipulation to succeed. These criteria serve as determining factors that greatly enhance your effectiveness in the realm of manipulation. Following that, we will examine some of the most prevalent manipulation techniques in existence.

Requirements for Successful Manipulation

When it comes to manipulating people, you might be pondering how to enhance your ability to control others. There are several ways to ensure the success of your manipulation, and ultimately, three primary criteria must be met for your manipulative efforts to be effective. All three of these criteria must align to give you the best chance of influencing those around you. To achieve genuine success, you must excel at concealing your intentions, comprehending the vulnerabilities of others, and developing the ruthlessness to execute your manipulation without succumbing to guilt.

Concealing Intentions

The cardinal rule of manipulation dictates that you must master the art of concealing your intentions. Simply put, if you make your manipulation overtly evident to someone, you forfeit the power needed for successful manipulation. Awareness of your manipulative tactics diminishes their effectiveness. When individuals perceive your intentions, they become less susceptible to your persuasion. In such cases, you transition from manipulation to persuasion.

In the realm of manipulation, concealing your intentions is paramount. Imagine, for instance, that you wish your partner to perform a task you'd rather avoid, like doing the dishes. Instead of openly expressing your reluctance to do the dishes or asking your partner directly to do them, you opt for a different approach. You might sigh, grumble, and show reluctance when it comes to getting up. Your aim is to invoke your partner's empathy by subtly communicating your unhappiness or discomfort. You hope that by revealing your distress, your partner will volunteer to help, believing it's their choice driven by compassion. Consequently, you achieve your desired outcome without explicitly stating your request.

Understanding Vulnerabilities

To effectively control others, you must possess a profound understanding of their vulnerabilities. This understanding is essential because people have diverse susceptibilities. Some may be inclined to succumb to guilt, while others are highly empathetic and readily offer assistance to alleviate someone's distress. Some individuals may be too self-conscious to resist directives, while others crave attention and eagerly respond to offers of it. Identifying these vulnerabilities empowers you to exploit them effectively. By discerning which aspect of someone's vulnerability to target, you can often persuade them to act in a manner conducive to your objectives. They may believe that complying with your wishes is their only path to achieving their desires. Recognizing and manipulating these vulnerabilities reshapes their behavior, granting you the control you seek.

Ruthlessness

The final criterion for successful manipulation is the development of a degree of ruthlessness. Ruthlessness is essential if you aspire to influence or control another person's thoughts and feelings. The ability to shape their thoughts and behaviors is meaningful only when you can do so without succumbing to guilt.

Many individuals struggle with this aspect of manipulation. They find it challenging to act in ways that they would not want inflicted upon themselves. Some cannot bring themselves to exploit others, particularly if the means involve direct harm. Such moral qualms are incompatible with effective manipulation. Feeling remorse for your actions, especially when it might lead you to divulge your intentions, undermines your capacity to manipulate effectively. Success in manipulation demands the ability to disregard guilt and cultivate a detached ruthlessness towards the consequences of your actions.

Methods of Manipulation

Manipulation encompasses a myriad of techniques for exerting influence over others. Some people resort to deceit, while others rely on incessant displays of affection and adoration. These methods vary widely, with no fixed rule dictating the choice of technique. Nevertheless, all manipulation techniques can generally be categorized into five distinct groups. These techniques encompass positive reinforcement, negative reinforcement, partial reinforcement, punishment, and trauma. Understanding these five categories will provide insights into the mechanics of the manipulation techniques you encounter. While they may differ significantly, each technique boasts its unique effectiveness.

Positive Reinforcement

Positive reinforcement involves providing individuals with a positive reward or outcome when they exhibit desired behavior. It encourages them to persist in the behavior by linking it with favorable consequences. Positive reinforcement may manifest as praise, rewards, or other positive incentives. For example, offering your children an allowance for completing their weekly chores is a form of positive reinforcement. By employing positive reinforcement in manipulation, you motivate the other party to continue behaving in ways that align with your goals.

Negative Reinforcement

Negative reinforcement operates in contrast to positive reinforcement. It reinforces a behavior by removing something negative when the desired action is performed correctly. For instance, the promise of an additional day off work if you complete your weekly tasks before the deadline is a form of negative reinforcement. Negative reinforcement in manipulation often involves demonstrating that the individual will face less hardship or inconvenience if they comply with your wishes. This method encourages them to cooperate in pursuit of a more favorable outcome.

Partial Reinforcement

Partial reinforcement introduces inconsistency into the reinforcement process. It aims to instill doubt or insecurity in the individual, compelling them to take risks to attain the desired outcome. This method capitalizes on the unpredictability of rewards, driving the individual to chase the reward even more fervently. Partial reinforcement manipulates by maintaining uncertainty about when or if a reward will be granted. This approach can be compared to the tactics employed in gambling, where players persist in the hope of winning due to the belief that a reward is statistically imminent.

Punishment

Punishment entails introducing something negative into the situation to discourage undesired behavior. It can involve making the undesirable behavior uncomfortable or unpleasant until the individual complies with your wishes. Methods such as nagging or employing the silent treatment serve as examples of punishment. The goal of punishment is to make the opposing behavior undesirable enough to prompt compliance. By utilizing punishment effectively, you coerce the other person into yielding to your desires.

Trauma

The most extreme form of manipulation involves the infliction of trauma on the other person. These methods are often overtly abusive and include verbal abuse, explosive tempers, intimidation, or attempts to establish dominance. The aim is to create fear or intimidation, discouraging the individual from contradicting or challenging the manipulator. The manipulator strives to make the person so apprehensive of provoking or upsetting them that compliance becomes the safer choice. Repetition of these traumatic tactics increases the manipulator's control, and in some cases, even a single traumatic event can prove effective.

In summary, comprehending these five criteria will enhance your understanding of the manipulation techniques explored in this section. These techniques may differ widely, but each possesses its distinctive efficacy. We will delve into each type of reinforcement within this section, exploring the implications and applications of each method.

Positive Reinforcement

Positive reinforcement involves offering a positive stimulus or reward when someone engages in a desired behavior. It functions to reinforce the behavior by associating it with positive outcomes. Positive reinforcement can manifest as praise, rewards, or other favorable incentives. For instance, if you want your children to complete their chores, you might offer them an allowance as positive reinforcement. The goal is to motivate them to continue the desired behavior by linking it to positive consequences. This approach is commonly employed in manipulation, encouraging the other party to act in a manner that aligns with your objectives by

providing them with positive reinforcement in the form of affection, gifts, or other rewards when they comply.

Negative Reinforcement

Negative reinforcement operates in opposition to positive reinforcement. It reinforces a behavior by eliminating something negative when the desired action is performed correctly. For example, consider a scenario where you promise an extra day off work if an employee completes their weekly tasks ahead of schedule. The negative reinforcement in this situation is the removal of the requirement to work on that particular day, which is viewed as a negative aspect. Negative reinforcement in manipulation frequently involves demonstrating that the individual will experience less discomfort or inconvenience if they comply with your wishes. This method incentivizes cooperation by highlighting the benefits of aligning with your goals.

Partial Reinforcement

Partial reinforcement introduces variability into the reinforcement process. Its objective is to create doubt or insecurity in the individual, motivating them to take risks in pursuit of the desired outcome. Partial reinforcement relies on the unpredictability of rewards, encouraging the individual to pursue the reward more vigorously. This approach aims to maintain uncertainty about when or if a reward will be received. It shares similarities with strategies employed in gambling, where players persist in their endeavors, believing that a reward is statistically inevitable. Manipulation through partial reinforcement maintains uncertainty and encourages the individual to persevere in the hope of achieving the desired outcome.

Punishment

Punishment entails the introduction of negative consequences to deter undesirable behavior. It can involve making the undesired behavior uncomfortable or unpleasant until the individual complies with your wishes. Tactics such as nagging or employing the silent treatment are examples of punishment. The objective of punishment is to render the opposing behavior unattractive enough to prompt compliance. By employing punishment effectively, you compel the other person to yield to your desires by making the undesired behavior undesirable.

Trauma

The most extreme form of manipulation involves inflicting trauma on the other person. These methods are often overtly abusive and may include verbal abuse, explosive displays of anger, intimidation, or attempts to establish dominance. The goal is to instill fear or intimidation, discouraging the individual from challenging or opposing the manipulator. The manipulator aims to make the person so apprehensive of provoking or upsetting them that compliance becomes the safer and more preferable option. Repeated use of these traumatic tactics strengthens the manipulator's control, and in some cases, a single traumatic event can be highly effective.

In conclusion, understanding these five categories will deepen your comprehension of the manipulation techniques discussed in this section. While these techniques exhibit significant variations, each possesses its distinct effectiveness. We will explore each form of reinforcement in greater detail within this section, elucidating their implications and applications.

5

EMOTIONS AND MANIPULATION

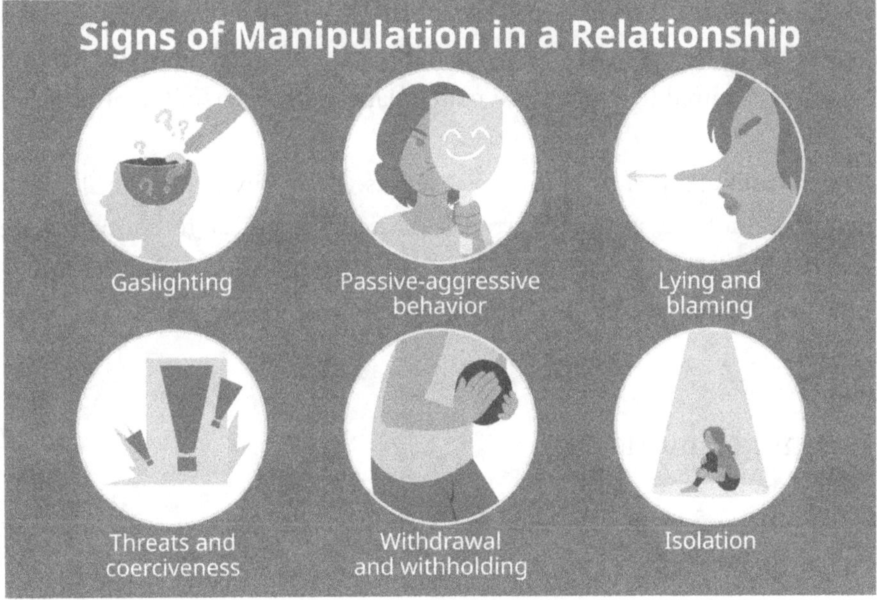

Ultimately, at the core of most manipulation lies the underlying emotion. Emotions present a challenge to contradict—most of the time, when you experience an emotion, it propels you into action. You often feel compelled to follow through, believing you have no alternative. This process frequently operates beneath your conscious awareness. Emotions serve as essential guides in life, motivating individuals in various ways.

However, it is precisely the mechanics of emotions that render them susceptible to manipulation. Emotions become targets for manipulation because they are easily influenced when others possess the knowledge and skills. By controlling these emotions, individuals can often manipulate and influence others in turn.

Within this chapter, we aim to gain a deeper understanding of emotions in general. We will closely examine what emotions are and their typical functioning in the lives of individuals. We will delve into their nature, exploring how they stimulate people into action. Lastly, we will explore the steps required to control and manipulate another person's emotions.

Understanding this chapter is crucial because the ability to manipulate other people's emotions ultimately translates into the power to control those individuals. It is vital to grasp how to control emotions first and recognize how this control can serve your interests and objectives.

Defining Emotions

Emotions, if we were to provide a definition, can be described as automatic and instinctive states of mind. By this definition, they occur spontaneously, often emanating from the unconscious mind. Your mind consists of two facets—the conscious aspect, which is susceptible to direct influence and control, and the unconscious mind, operating beyond your immediate awareness. Both are powerful components of your mind, each serving distinct yet equally important purposes.

Your conscious mind is the part you are consciously aware of. Everything you think, feel, and perceive belongs to your conscious mind—it encompasses your current awareness. Right now, your conscious mind is likely absorbed in reading these words. The unconscious mind operates continually in the background, managing essential functions while your conscious mind focuses on immediate tasks. This allows your conscious mind to avoid dealing with irrelevant matters, although they might become relevant in the future. These processes enable you to filter out what's important and what isn't, facilitating better overall processing.

Returning to emotions, they are entirely unconscious. They arise without your conscious input or direction. Whether positive or negative, emotions exist to influence how you respond to the world around you. They guide your behaviors directly, as we will explore shortly. Essentially, your mind processes its surroundings automatically and responds reflexively by generating an emotion. This is the primary means by which your unconscious mind can interact with the world—it influences you to behave.

In general, there are six fundamental emotions believed to underpin all others. These six emotions are experienced and exhibited universally, forming the basis for a wide range of emotional responses. These emotions are:

1. **Happiness:** This emotion serves as a reward for beneficial actions, encouraging their repetition. Happiness stems from behaviors that support your survival and well-being, such as consuming nourishing foods, engaging in physical exercise, and participating in sexual activities.

2. **Sadness:** In contrast to happiness, sadness discourages the repetition of harmful behaviors. It signals the recognition that certain actions have led to loss or harm in some way, aiming to prevent their recurrence.

3. **Anger:** Anger prepares you for a fight response when you perceive a threat or danger. It readies you to defend yourself if necessary, acting as a misunderstood yet vital emotion.

4. Fear: Fear arises when you sense a threat, leading to heightened alertness and awareness. It aids in your ability to respond defensively when needed, ultimately enhancing your chances of survival.

5. Surprise: Surprise emerges when something appears incongruent with your expectations, prompting further attention to understand its implications and influence on your response.

6. Disgust: This emotion arises when you encounter something potentially harmful to your physical or mental well-being, such as rotting or toxic substances.

The Role of Emotions in Driving Actions

In essence, the emotions you experience serve as potent motivators with a significant purpose: enabling you to respond effectively to your surroundings. They act as a bridge for your unconscious mind to communicate directly with your body, compelling you to take specific actions. Often, when dealing with your emotions, you may feel compelled to act in precise ways. For instance, anger might drive you to consider physically confronting someone, while sadness could prompt a desire to withdraw and recuperate away from others.

Regardless of how you react to your emotions, their fundamental function remains consistent: shaping your behaviors. This is mainly because everything you do, feel, and think is intricately interconnected. Your thoughts wield considerable influence in this context, as they invariably color your emotions. Consider this: if you harbor negative thoughts about dogs due to a childhood dog bite, encountering a dog will naturally trigger negative emotions. The initial thought shapes your feelings toward the dog, likely evoking fear directly attributed to that initial thought.

When fear grips you, your body responds accordingly. Your heart rate quickens, your breaths become shallower, and you feel alert and prepared to flee if necessary. These physiological responses occur because you believe there may be a need to escape or confront potential threats associated with the sight of a dog, as per your initial thought.

It's crucial to remember that if you aim to influence people, the most effective route often involves controlling their emotions. Primarily, this control hinges on targeting their thoughts directly.

Manipulating Emotions

Emotions, being unconscious and profoundly motivating, are surprisingly susceptible to manipulation. Given their unconscious nature, many individuals may not comprehend why they feel a certain way. They might fail to identify the root cause of their discomfort or stress, making them easily controllable. The disconnect between thoughts and feelings leaves numerous people vulnerable to manipulation. When you decide to manipulate emotions, the process is relatively straightforward. While a few essential steps are involved, once you grasp them, you'll find the manipulation process remarkably uncomplicated.

Step 1: Identify the Vulnerability

To commence, the first step involves pinpointing the vulnerability of the other party that you wish to manage. Your objective is to uncover the driving force behind their actions that you can exert control over. You are seeking avenues through which you can influence the other person to determine your best chances of success. Often, this initial step can prove to be quite challenging, especially if you lack a deep understanding of the individual you intend to influence. For instance, imagine you are a salesperson striving to secure a deal. In such scenarios, you usually have limited time to discern the motivators of the other party or devise means of exerting control. This isn't a shortcoming on your part; rather, it is a fundamental aspect of the profession and its dynamics.

Nevertheless, in this line of work, you must become proficient at swiftly identifying these vulnerabilities that can be easily harnessed. The vulnerabilities to focus on largely depend on the specific individual you are dealing with. Is the person you're conversing with a parent of young children? Often, you can leverage their concerns as new parents to guide them toward the actions you desire. Are they susceptible to someone displaying greater intelligence? Establish your authority as a knowledgeable figure.

Step 2: Evoke the Emotion

Once you have ascertained the vulnerability you intend to exploit, it's time to trigger the corresponding emotion. You may achieve this through conversation, utilizing implications about their actions or your opinions to introduce doubt into the other person's mind. Regardless of your approach, one principle remains constant: by eliciting the emotion, you should gain the ability to begin influencing their behavior.

Step 3: Manipulate

When the targeted emotion is triggered, you should observe the individual starting to behave in the manner you had anticipated. If you notice a shift in their actions, you can then proceed to reinforce those behaviors. You can persistently trigger the emotion to sustain the advantages it initially offered, thus maintaining your control over the other person.

6

HOW MANIPULATION WORKS

Ultimately, manipulation is effective because it seizes control over two fundamental drivers: exploiting vulnerabilities and tapping into people's needs. Most of the time, manipulation capitalizes on these aspects to trigger emotional reactions and fulfill those needs. When it successfully exploits a vulnerability or fulfills a need, it gains better control over the required reactions. People tend to be remarkably predictable in how they respond to the world, and identifying the right vulnerabilities or needs to exploit often leads to obtaining the desired outcomes.

In this chapter, we will explore these various vulnerabilities and needs. It's important to note that this list is not exhaustive; there are other vulnerabilities and needs out there. However, these are the most common ones you are likely to encounter.

Vulnerabilities to Exploit

Individuals possess various vulnerabilities that make them more susceptible to manipulation. If you intend to manipulate someone, watch for these common indicators that suggest an individual is easily exploitable and controllable.

1. Eagerness to Please
Some people take their desire to make others happy to an extreme. They feel compelled to take responsibility for everyone's happiness, often disregarding the cost to themselves. Their sense of self-worth hinges on their ability to please others, and they act accordingly, even if it means sacrificing their own well-being.

2. Fear of Negative Emotions
A common vulnerability is the fear of strong negative emotions. These individuals find it challenging to deal with negativity and prefer to avoid it by going along with what others want, even if it means making the wrong choices.

3. Lack of Assertiveness
Some people struggle to say no or stand up for themselves due to fear or a lack of confidence. They'd rather endure negativity than confront someone else.

4. Low Self-Esteem

People with low self-esteem have difficulty trusting themselves and often defer to others' judgments and decisions, making them easy targets for manipulation.

5. Lack of Boundaries

When individuals lack personal boundaries, they are more vulnerable to manipulation because they don't see a problem with others attempting to control them.

6. Naiveté

Naive individuals tend to take people at face value, making them easy targets for manipulation as they don't question others' intentions.

7. Giving the Benefit of the Doubt

Some individuals consistently give others the benefit of the doubt, making it easier for manipulators to deceive them.

8. Lack of Self-Confidence

Those lacking self-confidence are more prone to manipulation as they often believe they are wrong and don't defend themselves.

9. Overthinking

Overthinking can lead individuals to rationalize manipulation and downplay its significance, making them susceptible to control.

10. Submissive Personality

Naturally submissive people are more likely to acquiesce to manipulation, either due to codependency or a sense of worthlessness.

Needs to Exploit

In most cases, these vulnerabilities are driven by one of two core needs: the need to be right and the need to be accepted. These needs are what make people susceptible to manipulation in the first place and drive social influence.

1. The Need to Be Right

This is known as informational social influence, where people have a strong desire to be correct. When presented with evidence that they are wrong, they often shift their beliefs and behaviors to align with what they now perceive as correct.

2. The Need to Be Liked or Accepted

Humans are inherently social creatures, and the desire to be liked and accepted by others is a powerful motivator. People frequently conform to societal or peer pressure, making them susceptible to manipulation by those who exploit this need for social approval and conformity.

7

METHODS OF EMOTIONAL MANIPULATION

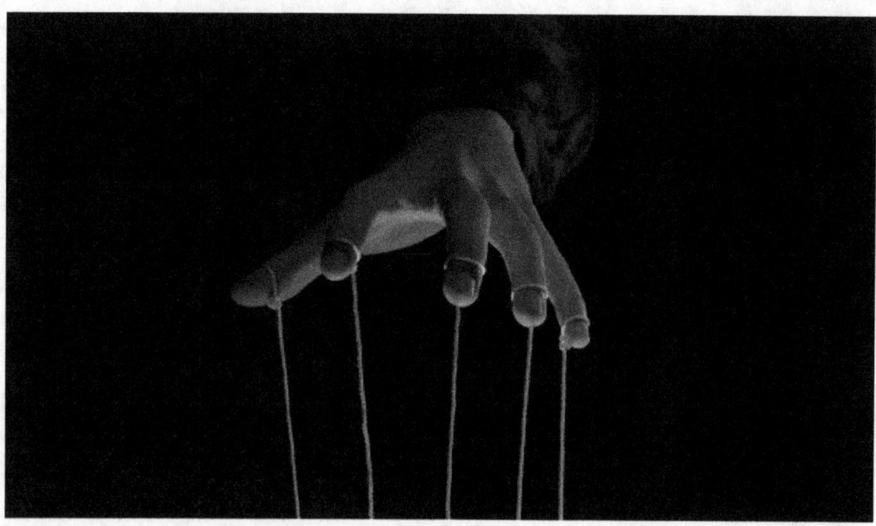

With all the necessary background information now covered, it's time to delve into the various ways manipulation can be employed. In this chapter, we will focus on exploring methods of emotional manipulation. We will begin by providing insight into what emotional manipulation entails. Subsequently, we will elucidate five distinct forms of manipulation that individuals can utilize to exert control over others. These methods, their mechanics, and the steps to effectively employ them will be thoroughly examined.

What Constitutes Emotional Manipulation?

Emotional manipulation hinges on harnessing someone else's emotions to facilitate control or influence over them. It entails seizing command of an individual's emotions and leveraging those emotions in any manner necessary to ensure compliance with one's desires. It is crucial to acknowledge that this is most frequently achieved by inducing feelings of uncertainty or self-doubt in people, with the intention of later assuming control over them. The objective is to guarantee that one achieves the desired outcomes promptly.

When delving into emotional manipulation, one essentially enters the psyche of another person. It involves employing psychological tactics to establish and manipulate emotions, allowing them to serve the manipulator's purposes.

In this chapter, we will present five distinct methods, although there are numerous others, demonstrating how gaslighting, minimizing, devaluation, playing the victim, and love bombing can be employed to gain control over someone and elicit desired actions.

Gaslighting

GASLIGHTING FEELS LIKE:

Among the methods discussed in this book, gaslighting stands out as one of the most sinister. Employing gaslighting enables one to dominate another person's mind. It is designed to erode the target's self-trust, leading them to trust the manipulator more than themselves. Essentially, it instills doubt in their ability to perceive the world around them accurately, rendering them vulnerable and dependent.

This method requires time to develop but can be incredibly potent when aiming to establish dependency or influence over another person. It is essential to recognize that gaslighting essentially dismantles a person's thought processes, undermining their trust and reducing them to a mere shadow of their former selves.

Step 1: Building Trust

The initial step in this process is establishing trust. The manipulator must be perceived as entirely trustworthy and respectable by the target. This often necessitates time and the cultivation of a dependable relationship. It is crucial to appear trustworthy to the people around, particularly the individual you intend to manipulate. Building genuine affection and excitement toward you is vital, as it leads them to not only trust but also love you. Love fosters a willingness to endure more than they otherwise might.

Step 2: Cataloging Mistakes

Simultaneous with building trust, it is crucial to meticulously record every mistake the target makes. By consistently highlighting their errors, no matter how minor, the manipulator ensures the target's continual self-doubt, making them more receptive to the manipulator's influence. Whenever the target begins to doubt themselves, the manipulator steps in to emphasize their mistakes, eventually compelling the target to accept their constant wrongness.

Step 3: Fostering Misunderstanding

After convincing the target of their fallibility, the manipulator must portray themselves as incapable of understanding the target's perspective, even when it is entirely logical. This involves refuting the target's valid viewpoints and supplying "correct" answers that serve the manipulator's agenda, all while presenting them as simple truths. The goal is to persuade the target that 2+2 equals 5, even when they know this is fundamentally false.

Step 4: Encouraging Forgetfulness

Continuing the manipulation, the manipulator begins to undermine the target's memory, causing them to doubt their own recollections. This is achieved by contradicting the target's accounts of minor details or events, leading them to eventually stop trusting their memory. The target starts readily accepting the manipulator's version of events whenever discrepancies arise.

Step 5: Downplaying Concerns

In the final step, the manipulator systematically belittles any concerns the target expresses regarding their memory or mental state. This tactic ensures the manipulation remains effective by diminishing the target's inclination to question the manipulator's actions or intentions. The overall aim of gaslighting is to make the target doubt themselves, favoring the manipulator's judgments and creating a reliance on the manipulator as the sole source of reality.

Minimizing

Another form of emotional manipulation is minimization. When employing this tactic, one endeavors to portray significant events as inconsequential or less significant than they truly are. This strategy is often employed to avoid consequences or discredit individuals voicing concerns or resisting the manipulator's actions. Minimization involves two key components that combine to minimize the importance of an event or situation.

Denial

The first component of minimization is denial. By refuting the severity of an event or situation, the manipulator convinces the target that their feelings of concern or hurt are unwarranted. For instance, if the target expresses frustration over the manipulator's inattentiveness, the manipulator may counter by asserting that the target is overly sensitive, thus negating the validity of their feelings.

Rationalization

The second component of minimization is rationalization. Here, the manipulator offers a plausible explanation for the situation that is difficult to refute rationally. For instance, if the target complains about the manipulator's emotional absence, the manipulator may attribute it to being preoccupied with work, a reason that cannot be logically argued against. This combination of denial and rationalization leaves the target feeling discredited and without a basis for their concerns.

Devaluation

Devaluation represents another common form of emotional manipulation. Its purpose is to make the target believe they are less valuable to the manipulator. This tactic is often employed in conjunction with intermittent reinforcement, creating a cycle where the target strives to regain the manipulator's affection, even if it means acting against their own values.

Devaluation primarily involves gradually withdrawing emotional support and attention. The manipulator ceases to rely on the target, reduces their own outreach, and refrains from showering the target with previous affection.

Playing the Victim

Playing the victim is a manipulation method employed when the target begins to suspect they are being manipulated and tries to expose it. This tactic involves reversing roles to put the target on the defensive and divert attention from the manipulator's actions.

This method involves three stages: deny, attack, and reverse victim and offender (DARVO).

Deny

In this stage, the manipulator vehemently denies any manipulation or wrongdoing, insisting that the accusations are entirely baseless.

Attack

Next, the manipulator shifts the focus by attacking the target, asserting that they are the actual abuser or offender in the situation. This attack serves to deflect attention away from the manipulator's actions.

Reverse Victim and Offender

In the final stage, the manipulator portrays themselves as the victim, emphasizing how they suffer due to the target's alleged abuse. This reversal makes the target so preoccupied with proving the manipulator wrong that they cease their efforts to uncover the manipulation.

Love Bombing

The final form of emotional manipulation we will explore is love bombing. Love bombing is a straightforward technique centered on convincing the target to love the manipulator. It revolves around associating the manipulator with positive feelings, often achieved through lavish displays of affection and gift-giving.

The manipulator aims to create an addiction within the target, making them believe that the manipulator is synonymous with happiness. By elevating the target's self-worth and showering them with extravagant gifts and praise, the manipulator fosters a sense of dependency and attachment. This idealized version of the manipulator becomes an addictive presence in the target's life.

Typically, love bombing is coupled with devaluation, forming a cycle where the target strives to maintain the manipulator's affection. As the target becomes addicted to the manipulator's idealized image, the manipulator can gradually withdraw these displays of affection and control the target's actions through emotional dependency.

In conclusion, emotional manipulation encompasses various tactics aimed at controlling others' emotions and actions. The methods discussed—gaslighting, minimizing, devaluation, playing the victim, and love bombing—illustrate different approaches to achieving this goal. Understanding these techniques is crucial for recognizing and protecting oneself from emotional manipulation.

8

METHODS OF MIND CONTROL

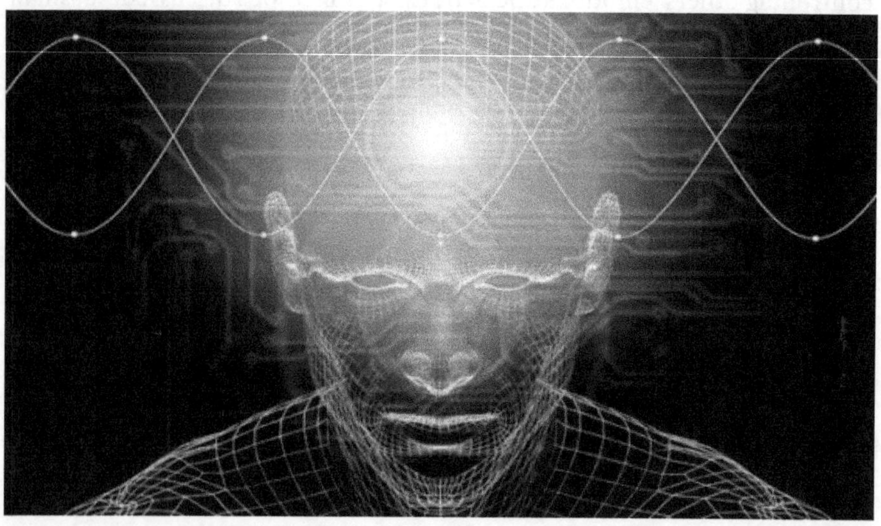

Have you ever desired the ability, by the day's end, to influence minds? Has there been a moment when you looked at someone and thought how much simpler and better things would be if you could steer their thoughts, their thought processes, and their actions? Perhaps you wish you could place a controller of thoughts in their minds, or maybe you wish to wield greater influence over those in your surroundings.

The reality is, you can achieve this. You can guide how people think and act. It may not be a precise science, as nothing in life ever is, but the fact remains that you can effortlessly control anyone. You can learn to manage what people think, how they think, and more. You can enhance your ability to discern how your actions influence others, and by understanding how your actions affect everyone around you, you can accomplish significant feats. You can shape the beliefs of people around you. You can subtly guide their thoughts, gradually pushing out external influences until, ultimately, you can assert complete control.

In this chapter, we will delve into the techniques of employing mind control. We will explore the ways in which you can ensure that, at the day's end, you are the one in charge. The ability to influence what others do becomes a potent means of control. You can meticulously shape their minds, molding them into precisely what you desire. Little by little, step by step, you can manage how the other person perceives the world, ultimately gaining better control over everything.

We will discuss four techniques of mind control. We will examine isolation as a form of mind control. Subsequently, we will analyze how you can use criticism to assist in controlling the thought processes of others, instilling doubt and uncertainty, enabling you to influence what they are thinking. We will unveil the use of peer pressure, demonstrating how, by managing the reactions of everyone around the individual you wish to control, you can also influence the targeted individual. Finally, we will illustrate how you can use repetition to gradually and carefully introduce a thought, thereby gaining better control over everything.

Each of these techniques presented will have its own distinct and genuine methods of application. They all empower you to better control the thoughts of those around you. However, trust lies at the heart of all these techniques. You must cultivate the trust required to gain access to the other person's mind. The mind is a highly guarded aspect of an individual, and although it is susceptible to control and influence if you know what you are doing, trust is imperative to make it happen. You must be in a trusted position to be confident that what you are doing is right. It is only in that position of trust that you attain that power. Only when you are certain that you know what you are doing can you truly tap into the potential of other people's minds.

What is Mind Control?

Mind control is not what most people might initially conceive; it does not involve merely implanting a chip, casting a spell, or any other means in an attempt to influence how others perceive things. It does not grant you the power to exercise perfect control over someone else. You don't gain the ability to dictate someone's movements precisely as you wish. Instead, you can control other people through various methods.

There is no magical way to control someone like a robot. You cannot simply use a remote control to meticulously manage their actions. However, what you can do is alter their programming. Mind control, in the sense depicted here, is designed to help you gain better control over everything. It empowers you to introduce new programming. When you break it down, mental programming provides a more accurate representation of the most intrinsic functions.

You influence the mind to control behaviors. Ultimately, we are all slaves to a fundamental aspect of life: our thoughts dictate our emotions, and it is these emotions, these natural motivators, that influence how we act. This perpetual cycle of thoughts, feelings, and behaviors is ceaseless. It's a mechanism to make functioning in life easier than ever, allowing your body and mind to take shortcuts so you don't have to figure out how to better influence your behavior, promoting efficiency in actions that require close attention.

However, this constant interplay between the body and mind renders them exceedingly susceptible to exploitation. It doesn't take much effort to completely control how someone else behaves. All you need to do is implant your own thoughts into their mind. As they begin to adopt your thoughts, they will behave in the manner you desire. Essentially, the more control you exert over their thoughts, the more you can dictate how other people behave.

Isolation

The initial method of control is isolation. Reflect on it—when individuals are isolated, they begin to suffer. We are fundamentally social beings, craving social intimacy more than anything else. When you isolate someone, you take charge of their mind. In fact, numerous cults employ this method to control their members. By isolating people, they become more susceptible to influence. When individuals are isolated, they start feeling as if they have no option but to stay. They become more pliable over time if they are cut off from everyone else. Doubt starts to creep in, particularly when combined with other manipulative techniques like gaslighting, constantly filling the individual with uncertainty.

To isolate people, you must gradually and steadily build a relationship with them. You need to earn their trust, and to achieve that, you need a way to be either trusted or in control. Essentially, you need to position yourself into a position of authority using other techniques; you can use the principles of persuasion to establish yourself as an authoritative figure. You can leverage body language to influence people's thoughts. You can employ mirroring, a concept we'll introduce in Chapter 8: Neuro-Linguistic Programming in this book.

Once you are in a position of trust, it's time to systematically assert your point of view. It's time to gradually plant your thoughts, bit by bit. To isolate someone, you must quietly and cleverly convince them that nobody else matters. You subtly create rifts between them and those around them. You work to erase that sense of connection between your target and the people around them.

As you work on nurturing your relationship with the other person, you subtly persuade them to adopt your worldview. You cautiously talk to them, sowing the seeds of an idea within them. You educate them on what you want them to believe, using many of the other techniques. Isolation, in many ways, is the first step you must take to control minds. Once you have isolated the other person, you become the sole individual they interact with. You insert yourself into that trusted position, fostering an "us versus the world" mentality where you convince them that you have their best interests at heart and that you are desperately trying to take control of the situation. When they trust you and believe that you genuinely care about them and are committed to assisting them, their defenses come down.

It's when these defenses drop, when the individual is less concerned about whether you might pose a threat or not, that you can finally enter and alter their thoughts. There are various ways to achieve this. You could position yourself in that trusted role and continually alter the way you interact with the other person, modifying their thinking by repeating the points you wish to convey. You might provide subtle criticisms in the hopes that they internalize them and live by them, enabling you to better address the issue at hand. Perhaps you demonstrate to them that they need to follow what you're doing to fit in with you, employing peer pressure. Regardless of the method you choose, one thing remains true:

your trusted position, and your status as the sole individual in that trusted position, are what will empower you. When you establish that position of trust that grants you power, you become the only voice that matters because yours is the only one they hear.

Isolation commonly manifests in various forms, varying significantly from one situation to another. Some of these types include:

1. Physical isolation:
This entails restricting an individual's movement, keeping them close to you without allowing access to external resources and influences that could act as distractions. It could involve taking someone on a weekend getaway or keeping them at your home. It doesn't necessarily mean physically restraining someone; it can also involve monopolizing their time. The goal is to create physical distance between the individual and others.

2. Mental isolation:
When you isolate someone mentally, you make them feel alone. They may or may not actually be alone, but you set it up so that you have complete control over them. The longer you keep them alone and isolated from people, such as by blocking phone communication or intercepting letters, the more likely you are to control their mind. The longer you keep them alone or make

them feel like no one else cares, the more uncertain they become.

3. Censorship:

Another way, particularly in cults, that isolation can be employed is through censorship. If you can physically isolate someone and place them in a situation where they have no access to media, no access to what's happening in the world, and no access to any other way of perceiving the world, you can begin to control their thoughts. You might only expose them to messages that support your agenda. The more you do this, and the longer they go without receiving contradicting information, the more you can control their beliefs.

Critiquing

Critiquing involves an effort to manage and influence the environment around you. When you critique individuals, you gradually erode their confidence, subtly guiding them toward your desired outcome. Essentially, you manipulate the situation to make them feel responsible for change.

Criticism introduces doubt, often subtly and indirectly, cloaked beneath a veneer of plausible deniability. To employ criticism effectively, you must first discern the person's insecurities and identify their areas of vulnerability. This insight allows you to gradually chip away at their self-esteem.

For instance, imagine you want your partner to embark on self-improvement, whether it's losing weight, pursuing education, or seeking employment. You aim for them to become more engaging in social interactions. However, they show no interest in change.

In this scenario, your task is to subtly sow seeds of self-doubt. You want them to recognize room for improvement. You want them to perceive their current state as problematic, prompting them to feel compelled to address the issue in some way. The more adeptly you achieve this, the likelier they are to align with your preferences.

For instance, if your goal is to persuade your partner to pursue education, you may casually mention how uneducated individuals might be seen as lazy. Gradually, you undermine the very aspect of them that you wish to change. Over time, their self-assurance wanes, and they begin to question themselves. Ultimately, criticism compels them to exert greater effort to gain recognition, yielding the desired outcome.

This strategy essentially employs shame, inducing feelings of inadequacy in the individual. The intention is to prompt them to shed the traits that hinder their personal growth, with the expectation that they will then comply with your wishes.

Peer Influence

Peer pressure represents another viable method for exerting control over others. To shape someone's mindset, surround them with individuals who exhibit the desired behaviors. The more you demonstrate that everyone else is engaged in a particular activity, the greater the pressure for conformity. This compliance is a critical aspect to consider when employing this method. When harnessed effectively, peer pressure convinces people to make the changes you seek.

Consider how teenagers often readily conform to social expectations to fit in, gain approval, and experience a sense of belonging. This desire is profound—they believe they must conform to be liked. Consequently, they engage in activities they may not truly desire, resulting in collective discomfort as everyone complies merely to appear responsible.

When you utilize peer pressure, you aim to either make yourself engage in the desired behavior or bring others into the fold who will. Alternatively, you might convince the target individual that people they identify with already embrace the desired behavior. By highlighting how those relevant to the individual endorse the behavior, you imply that conformity is necessary to fit in.

Achieving this is relatively straightforward. You consistently reference how people the target person can relate to are already engaged in the behavior you advocate. You emphasize the ubiquity of these actions. As pressure mounts on the individual, they gradually become more persuasive. Eventually, they feel compelled to conform, driven by the overwhelming urge to be part of the group, leading to the uncomfortable situation of following suit, not out of personal desire but to maintain a sense of belonging.

Repetition

Lastly, employing repetition is a method to control someone's mindset. The human mind is ever-attentive, especially the subconscious, which constantly absorbs and processes its surroundings on a grand scale. It attentively processes the environment so your conscious mind doesn't have to. It indiscriminately takes in information and stimuli, forming the basis for subliminal manipulation, an avenue through which you can influence the subconscious.

One way to mold the subconscious is through persistent repetition. Re-iterating a point consistently allows it to be internalized gradually. Over time, the idea gains perceived validity, accepted almost unquestioningly. You find yourself paying attention to this point because you've encountered it repeatedly.

Think about how you've absorbed life lessons by hearing your parents repeatedly discuss them. How many beliefs and ideas have you adopted simply because you've heard someone assert them persistently? Many people aren't aware of how easily they can be influenced, a fact made evident by the effectiveness of advertising. You may tune out advertisements, but subconsciously, they still affect your choices. When deciding which brand to choose, you instinctively gravitate toward the one you've been exposed to the most, a bias cultivated through relentless exposure to advertising.

Similarly, when you aim to control someone else's mind, subtly reiterate your points. Address the same topic multiple times in various contexts and settings, endeavoring to make the individual believe your perspective is their own. You strive to change their thought patterns constantly, effortlessly integrating your new subject into discussions.

For instance, if you believe in the importance of education, subtly and discreetly steer conversations towards this theme. The key is to make the individual feel like these thoughts are their own, preventing them from sensing coercion. You want them to reach conclusions independently, ensuring you remain unattributed for their transformation.

Next time, find ways to introduce your ideas without drawing attention. It could be a single word or concept. For instance, if you desire Italian food for dinner, engage in conversations about Mediterranean cuisine, pasta, or Rome, and then casually ask what the other person wants for dinner. By planting the idea in their subconscious, they gradually adopt the desired thought patterns. Over time, you master the art of influencing their mind discreetly and effectively, all while remaining unnoticed.

9

USING EURO-LINGUISTIC PROGRAMMING

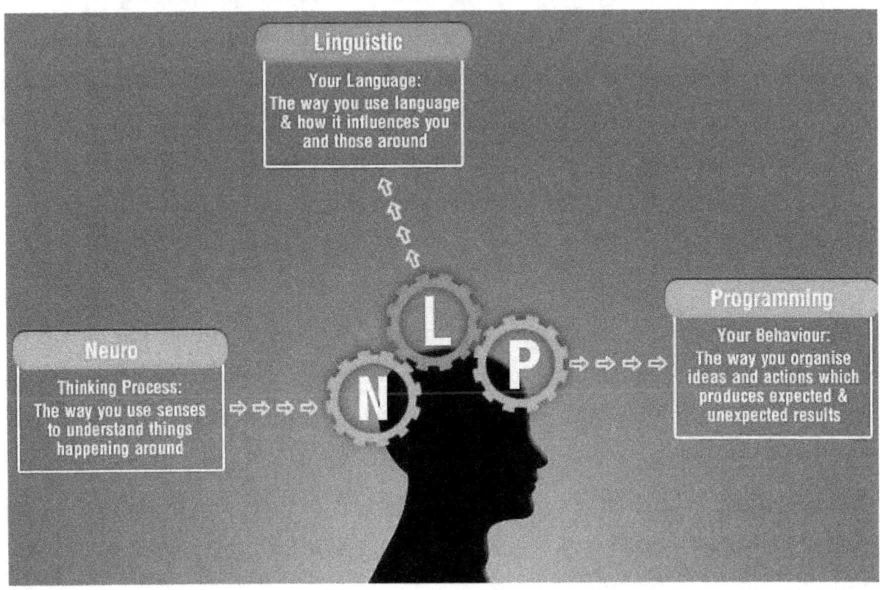

Beneath many effective strategies for exerting control or influence over others lie a set of fundamental principles that pertain to

51

human behavior. These principles, known as the principles of persuasion, provide a framework for shaping the thoughts and actions of individuals. Unlike many other methods discussed in this book, these principles are transparent in their approach. When you engage in persuasion, those you seek to influence are fully aware of your intentions because you directly communicate your desires to them. However, it's important to note that openly acknowledging your use of these methods can diminish their effectiveness. The power of persuasion lies not in the words themselves but in how the human mind responds to them.

Persuasion is an immensely potent tool that enables you to craft your messages in a compelling manner, increasing the likelihood of others aligning with your perspective. It empowers you to navigate the world more effectively by harnessing the influence of your words.

In this chapter, we will delve into the art of persuading people, exploring the essence of persuasion itself. This is a crucial concept that can be applied in nearly any context. To be influential and successful, one must master the art of persuasion. Those who excel in this skill can skillfully phrase their requests in a manner that encourages voluntary compliance. People willingly cooperate because they believe in the reasons provided to them, not because they are coerced.

If you are pursuing a career in sales, this skill set is indispensable. It can be perceived as manipulative since it allows you to leverage these principles effectively, essentially guiding someone else's thoughts. Nevertheless, it's crucial to recognize that these methods have valid applications beyond manipulation. They serve as legitimate tools for convincing others to align with your objectives. Persuading people to take certain actions is a legitimate and not always harmful endeavor.

Persuasion can be viewed from two perspectives: through the lens of the principles of persuasion, consisting of six powerful principles that directly influence the human mind, and within the context of rhetoric, the formalized art of persuasive communication dating back to the philosopher Aristotle.

Principles of Persuasion

The six principles of persuasion provide a means to directly influence someone's thoughts. They offer insights into becoming as compelling as possible. By employing these principles, you can encourage people to do what you desire. These principles operate on various subconscious levels, as individuals are typically unaware of how you are subtly altering their patterns of thinking. They do not perceive your deliberate efforts to change their minds or take control. In the end, it's your presentation and approach that enable you to wield influence while remaining transparent about your intentions. You provide the necessary information for them to make decisions while employing strategies to enhance your impact.

Reciprocity

The first principle we explore is reciprocity, the idea that when you do something for someone, they naturally feel inclined to reciprocate. It doesn't have to be a grand gesture; a simple act of kindness toward another person can elicit a desire to return the favor. For instance, imagine you are a car salesperson meeting with a potential client who has children. You might offer the children a lollipop or a snack to keep them content. The parents observe this display of goodwill, and subconsciously, they feel compelled to reciprocate in some way. Does this mean they'll buy a car solely because of a lollipop? Not necessarily, but you position yourself as more deserving of their consideration. They are more likely to want to give back to you because you've given to them and their family.

Reciprocity is a commonly used principle in various contexts, such as promotional offers that entice you to sign up with the promise of a gift. Harnessing the power of reciprocity taps into a fundamental aspect of human nature. As social beings, we naturally engage in reciprocity, which benefits our survival as a species. When you help others, they are more likely to help you in return, ensuring the collective survival and prosperity of the group.

Consistency and Commitment

Consistency is a quality we all value because it provides predictability and reliability. When individuals demonstrate commitment and consistency, we tend to adopt these traits ourselves. However, this can make us predictable. This principle capitalizes on that fact, suggesting that once you get someone to commit to something, even if it's small or seemingly insignificant, you can usually get them to agree to more substantial requests in the future. By securing a small commitment initially, you set the stage for further cooperation.

To employ this principle effectively, you start by getting someone to agree to something minor before making your main request. For example, if you want someone to work late for you, allowing you to leave early, begin by securing a small commitment, such as asking them to assist with a quick task at work. This initial agreement puts them in a cooperative mindset, making it easier to build on and make more substantial requests. Once they've agreed to help with something small, you've primed them for greater cooperation.

In conclusion, these principles of persuasion can be powerful tools when used judiciously. They provide a framework for influencing others while maintaining transparency and ethical conduct. By understanding and applying these principles, you can enhance your ability to navigate various situations and achieve your objectives effectively.

Social Validation

We find ourselves once again at a fundamental concept that has been repeatedly emphasized throughout this book—the innate human inclination to conform with the actions of others. Social validation essentially involves persuading someone to comply with your request for social reasons. It entails applying peer pressure, essentially inducing them to believe that the entire group is engaging in a particular behavior. This phenomenon explains why, when something becomes popular, more and more individuals naturally gravitate towards it. You can observe this in high schools and shopping malls alike, where people tend to adopt the same fashion trends, whether they genuinely like them or not. When something is deemed trendy, it becomes a collective pursuit, and individuals feel compelled to keep up with the group. Consequently, individuals often relinquish their autonomy and default to following the crowd because it's easier than taking a risk and potentially not fitting in.

Because people inherently desire acceptance and a sense of belonging, this principle is consistently effective. Unless you are dealing with individuals who consciously defy societal norms, you can generally rely on this principle to yield results.

Suppose you are trying to persuade someone to sign a petition. In that case, you may heavily emphasize how everyone in the neighborhood has already agreed to it or highlight the endorsements of influential figures who support the petition's cause. You might mention that others in the person's demographic are frequently adopting a particular product to encourage them to do the same. Commercials also employ this tactic, often depicting new mothers cuddling their newborns and asserting that both mothers and hospitals endorse a product.

To apply this principle yourself, identify the social group to which your target belongs and appeal to that sense of belonging. Demonstrate how others in a similar position are already doing what you're proposing. By doing this consistently, you can typically persuade the person to agree.

Authority

Appealing to authority is perhaps one of the simplest principles to leverage. All you need to do is establish yourself as an expert or an authority in a particular field or context. If you can demonstrate why people should listen to you, you can usually persuade them to do so. Consider this scenario: if you needed medical advice, would you rely on the guidance of the receptionist, the nurse, or the doctor? Most individuals would place more trust in the doctor's advice, irrespective of whether it is accurate or not. This preference arises because people tend to assume that the doctor possesses the most expertise, which is often the case.

To drive this point home, think about a situation where you or your partner is pregnant. Would you prioritize the advice of an obstetrician or a podiatrist regarding what the pregnant woman should do? Most people would naturally turn to the obstetrician. It's because they see no reason not to trust the expert in that particular field. People consistently gravitate towards those with the most experience, regardless of the domain.

To apply this principle, establish in some way that you are an expert. There are various ways to do this. For instance, you could display your diploma in your office, showcasing your degree in a relevant field. You might choose to exhibit photographs of satisfied clients enjoying the benefits of your services. Or you could post a sign in your lobby, proudly announcing the number of people you've helped. Essentially, you want to convey that you possess the experience necessary to justify being the one people should listen to. By accomplishing this, you will often find it easier to persuade those around you to heed your advice.

Liking

This concept may appear unusual at first, but it actually follows a logical pattern. The more likable you are, the more likely people will view you as trustworthy and persuasive. When you try to persuade someone who already likes you, they are more inclined to agree with you compared to someone who doesn't hold the same positive feelings towards you. This phenomenon is influenced by our subtle inclinations. It's essential to realize that being likable increases the likelihood of receiving assistance from others.

People tend to gravitate towards helping those they like, and there's a specific reason behind this. When we like someone, we believe we share common ground with them. It could be a similarity or a sense of relatability. However, it's crucial to recognize that this can be easily manipulated without much effort.

To harness this principle, all you need to do is make yourself likable. If you're interacting with a stranger, find ways to establish a connection that makes you more relatable. This is why icebreakers are often used in meetings or negotiations – they create a more open atmosphere, allowing better interaction among participants.

To become more likable, consider these three points during your interactions with others:

1. **Humanize yourself** – Display personal photos in your office, share personal anecdotes, or find common interests to discuss. If you notice they're wearing a football shirt, find a way to relate to it. If they have young children and you do too, share that common experience. These strategies help you establish rapport and come across as more likable.

2. **Boost their self**-esteem – People naturally favor individuals who make them feel good about themselves. You can achieve this by offering sincere

compliments or finding ways to relate to their interests and choices. Whether you admire their hairstyle or appreciate their choice of a car, ensure your compliments are genuine. Authenticity is crucial; insincerity is easily detected and defeats the purpose.

3. Foster cooperation – Emphasize the idea of working together as a team with a shared goal. By reinforcing the notion that you are both part of a cooperative effort, you remind them that you are on their side. This alignment fosters positive feelings towards you. This is why phrases like "Help me help you" have gained popularity.

Scarcity

The final principle to take into account is the concept of scarcity. Whenever something is considered scarce, its value invariably rises. Human inclination leans towards items that aren't abundantly available. If something is labeled as scarce and, therefore, valuable, it tends to attract a swarm of attention. This phenomenon is frequently observed; people frequently pursue the latest limited supply or limited edition products. Their desire isn't driven by genuine need; rather, it's fueled by the item's popularity. Consider how numerous fast-food chains and cafes employ this strategy. They frequently introduce seasonal items, often so successfully that the product itself becomes a trend, like pumpkin spice dominating the market from early August to Thanksgiving. The high demand for this flavor is fueled by its limited availability during that specific season, causing its market presence to expand significantly. What was once just a coffee flavor can now be found in cookies, candles, perfumes, cereals, oatmeal, and nearly every other baked good or treat. Its worth skyrocketed because it was limited and coveted by everyone. There are always long lines for the first pumpkin spice latte at the beginning of the season. Similarly, when something else is scarce, such as a limited edition item, it will always be highly sought after. Its value soars, not because it's genuinely popular, but because it's scarce.

To apply this principle yourself, you must find a way to present your actions or offers to others as scarce. This concept is applicable in relationships as well, as seen in the ultimatum: "Do this, or I'm ending the relationship." By employing this ultimatum, you create a sense of scarcity around yourself. Suddenly, you become a sought-after commodity due to the genuine threat of your absence. The notion of not being able to attain something in the future increases its desirability. People naturally desire it more because it's not guaranteed.

Persuasion

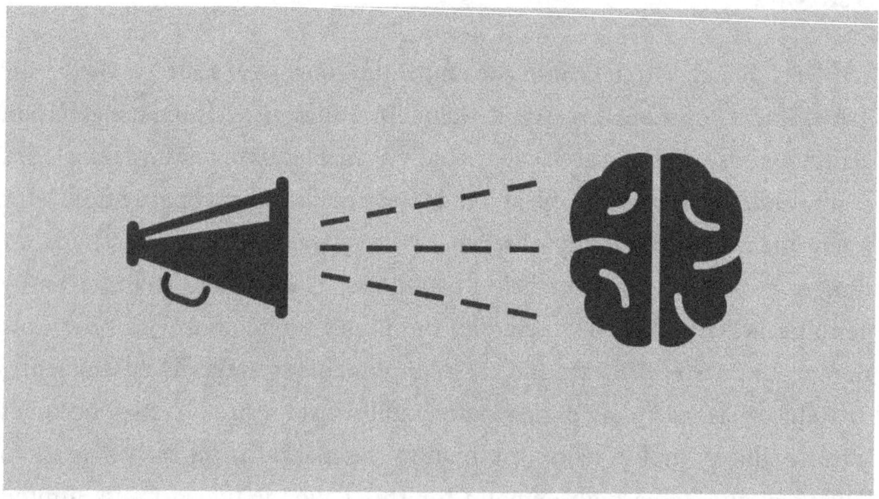

Another approach to discussing persuasion is through the art of rhetoric. Rhetoric is a form of communication aimed at effectively influencing others. Its primary purpose is to craft language in a manner that convinces and motivates people to alter their beliefs or behaviors. It involves choosing the right words and strategies to ensure that, ultimately, everyone is persuaded by your message.

Rhetoric comprises three fundamental principles: appealing to authority or character, appealing to emotion, and appealing to logic. While these principles function somewhat differently, they all contribute to enhancing your persuasive abilities when integrated into your communication.

1. Appeal to authority or character

When seeking to appeal to someone's character or authority, you must portray them as inherently worth listening to in some way. It is crucial to present your message in a compelling manner, making a strong case for why you should be heeded. This may involve invoking an external authority, but it can also encompass discussing what personal qualities or experiences make you worthy of attention. For instance, you might highlight the aspects of your personality that contributed to your success in running a business or the challenges you overcame to reach your current position. By emphasizing these character traits, you can make a convincing case and increase the likelihood of others embracing your cause. This is often achieved by sharing compelling personal stories or experiences during interactions, demonstrating your competence and making yourself a more compelling figure to follow.

2. Appeal to emotion

An appeal to emotion aims to elicit powerful feelings in your target audience. To employ this strategy effectively, you inject elements into your narrative that trigger these emotions in the person you are trying to persuade. This can involve recounting unfortunate events that occurred to those who ignored your advice or attempting to put someone in a positive mood to gain their agreement. You may also make individuals more inclined to support a cause by showing them images of those who would benefit from their contribution.

Regardless of the specific method you use, it's important to note that negative emotions tend to be the most potent motivators. If you want someone to take action that leads to change, you must find ways to persuade them through these negative emotions. By prompting individuals to act in order to free themselves from negativity and maintain a positive state of mind, you can effectively encourage them to follow your lead.

3. Appeal to logic

Lastly, the appeal to logic involves persuading people through the use of facts and figures. The goal is to construct an argument so compelling that individuals cannot reject it. Often, however, the logic employed doesn't have to be airtight; you can inundate someone with statistics and numbers, creating the impression that you must be correct, even if that's not necessarily the case. This approach hinges on convincing people to act based on the assumption that your numerical data is sound, sparing them the effort of delving into the intricacies of your calculations.

This method typically relies on a profusion of numbers and mathematical information. If you can employ this technique, you may find that people around you become convinced not because you are unquestionably right, but because you sound convincing. Incorporating relevant statistics into your arguments can make them more compelling, as individuals often align with suggestions that appear grounded in factual data. People are naturally inclined to agree with persuasive tactics that seem to rely on facts when they believe the evidence supports a change in their behavior.

10

USING BODY LANGUAGE TO MANIPULATE

The last manipulation technique explored in this book pertains to the utilization of body language—a remarkably potent and compelling tool. Body language offers a multitude of avenues for directly influencing and exerting control over others. Due to its nonverbal nature and the predominance of the unconscious mind in governing it, people often remain oblivious to its manipulative use. They fail to recognize its influence because they do not consciously scrutinize the way others move. Instead, they instinctively experience gut reactions guiding their responses to their surroundings. These involuntary impulses drive them to act without a conscious understanding of why they feel compelled to do so.

When employing body language to manipulate others, one essentially taps into this unconscious predisposition. By comprehending how the unconscious mind operates, one gains the power to influence others. Recognizing that the unconscious mind constantly observes and engages, and is responsible for individuals' emotional responses, provides a strategic advantage. Exploiting this advantage can lead to altering the behaviors of those being influenced, unless the person possesses a high level of self-awareness regarding their own body language and attentiveness to modifying it.

The Influence of Body Language

Body language possesses remarkable influence, serving as a dominant means of communication between individuals. It is essential to realize that the majority of communication occurs nonverbally. Observing how people react underscores this fact. How you approach someone communicates volumes—approaching with a scowl, for example, is likely to provoke fear initially and, potentially, anger if they choose to retaliate. Your body language, along with how you carry and present yourself, significantly shapes the perception others have of you. Harnessing this power allows you to consistently exercise control over others, ensuring that they respond in the desired manner through your presentation.

Your movements naturally trigger the unconscious mind of the other person. These movements register and elicit feelings, which directly influence how the individual interacts with you. Through your demeanor and expressions, you can make someone feel inferior, at ease, fearful, submissive, or even attracted. Although mastering control over your body language may prove challenging initially, it empowers you to continually shape the reactions of those around you. While not foolproof, you can typically orchestrate these reactions.

Body Language for Leadership

Leaders typically exude confidence through their body language. If your goal is to lead a group or be perceived as a competent leader, projecting confidence is paramount. Confidence and leadership are closely intertwined, as confidence is commonly associated with trustworthiness. To align your body language with that of a leader, consider implementing the following changes:

1. Maintain Eye Contact:

Engaging with others through confident eye contact is essential. However, it's crucial that your eye contact does not come across as dominating or overpowering. The aim is not to intimidate but to establish rapport and convey active listening.

2. Stand Tall:

Confidence is expressed through your posture. Stand tall and maintain a level head. Keep your spine straight without tilting your head back, always maintaining direct eye contact.

3. Release Tension:

Tension signals nervousness, while assertive calmness requires the release of tension. Demonstrating control is key to appearing confident.

4. Open Body Language:

Maintain open body language by avoiding crossed arms, crossed legs, or hiding behind objects. Remove barriers between yourself and others.

5. Gesture While Talking:

Use your hands while speaking to appear engaged and prevent nervous fidgeting. Still or hidden hands suggest secrecy or discomfort, which can undermine your confident image.

Expressing Dominance Through Body Language

Another form of body language worth considering is dominant body language. This non-verbal communication style can be employed to exert influence and assert authority over those in your vicinity. It serves as a means to convey your control and position at the top of the hierarchy, whether you are seeking to establish dominance at home, in the workplace, or elsewhere. To effectively dominate others, there are straightforward body language guidelines to follow, ensuring that you remain in command of the situation.

A significant aspect of dominant body language involves maximizing your physical presence. When you dominate a space, you occupy it entirely, sending a clear message that you are the one in control. By doing so, you communicate that your significance surpasses that of others, and you expect to have your desires and preferences respected.

Widening your stance is a key technique in this regard. The wider your stance, the more self-assured you appear, and any stance exceeding shoulder-width is immediately perceived as dominant. Dominance, in essence, goes beyond mere confidence; it signifies your complete control over a situation, with the power to make all decisions. Stand as widely and tall as possible to project the image of someone fully capable of directing their surroundings.

Placing your hands on your hips is another effective move. This action naturally extends your arms, making you appear larger, akin to a cobra spreading its hood or animals puffing up to appear more imposing. This expansion of your physical presence conveys dominance and control.

Maintaining a head-up, chin-high posture is equally crucial. Holding your head up and positioning your chin prominently conveys your authority. By widening your stance, you create the illusion of height and the ability to look down on others, even if you are physically shorter. This subtle visual cue reinforces your dominance.

Elevating your physical position is a common tactic to establish dominance. Ensuring that you are situated higher than everyone else around you, whether by using a taller chair or selecting the highest seat at the table, instantly places you in a dominant position. When others must look up to you, whether consciously or unconsciously, you are automatically perceived as more dominant.

Expanding your territorial claim is another strategy. Whenever possible, occupy more space than what is traditionally allotted to you. Encroach slightly on the personal space of others, refusing to make concessions. This gesture signifies your dominance by virtue of the extra space you assert in the environment.

Physical touch plays a pivotal role in declaring dominance. Touching another person, such as a firm grip on their arm or maintaining a handshake after they have released it, demonstrates your control. Likewise, patting someone on the shoulder or back as they pass by reinforces your authority, signaling your dominance in that particular interaction. Touching their belongings also signifies possession, indicating your readiness to transgress social norms and personal boundaries.

Walking in the center of a shared space without yielding is a powerful statement of dominance. In customary encounters where two individuals approach each other on a sidewalk or a street, the polite course of action is to make space for the other person, signifying respect. However, when asserting dominance, you refuse to relinquish any space, claiming it solely for yourself.

Finally, the power of a stare, especially when intense and unwavering, should not be underestimated. It ranks among the most potent methods for asserting dominance within a group. A prolonged and focused gaze tends to make others uncomfortable, and this discomfort is entirely intentional. Staring with a neutral or mildly displeased expression allows you to establish a sense of dominance over the other person, creating your sphere of influence through the intensity of your gaze.

Body Language to Attract

Using your body language effectively can be a powerful tool when it comes to attracting someone. Whether you're interested in a physical or romantic connection, a simple glance and the way you carry yourself can subtly convey your intentions. The key is to present yourself in a way that encourages reciprocity without appearing overly assertive. Regardless of your desired type of relationship, there are unmistakable signals you can employ to effectively communicate your interest. It's important to note that the body language discussed here is generally applicable to both genders.

11

CONCLUSION

And now, you've reached the conclusion of the book on Manipulation. Hopefully, as you've delved into these pages, you've discovered a comprehensive guide on how to effectively influence others. Remember, as you've absorbed the content, you've been presented with a plethora of techniques to shape the behaviors of individuals. You've only scratched the surface of the numerous methods available and the diverse approaches to controlling others. This book has unveiled a world you can harness to your advantage, provided you understand how to wield it. With the knowledge you've gained, you can begin influencing virtually anyone in your life effortlessly.

Throughout the text, you've been guided through various strategies for gaining control over others. You're now aware of the astonishing vulnerability of the human mind and how easily it can be influenced. The human psyche is far from impervious, as demonstrated by the simple act of altering your behavior and approach when dealing with others.

Remember that underlying all these processes is a fundamental principle: thoughts trigger emotions, emotions drive actions, which, in turn, generate more thoughts. To exercise control over others, you must recognize that, ultimately, you're the one in control. You must be prepared to step in and disrupt this cycle within people if necessary. Maintain a discreet presence to avoid detection by others. Always strive to master your own behavior, knowing that by doing so, you enhance your control over others.

From this point forward, remember that you should only manipulate others if you're willing to accept the consequences. Do not tamper with people's minds if you're not prepared to take responsibility for your actions or uncertain about the outcomes. Understand that meddling with people's thoughts and emotions can be perilous, and you must keep this in mind. As you utilize the methods provided in this book, always consider the potential aftermath of your actions. Reflect on how you could bring about significant change if you employ these methods in different ways. Remind yourself that, ultimately, you determine the nature of your interactions and bear responsibility for the outcomes.

Thank you for dedicating your time to read this book, and I appreciate your reaching its conclusion. If you've found this book valuable, please consider visiting Amazon today to leave a review!

9 783988 317742